WE ARE ALL DIFFERENT

A CELEBRATION OF DIVERSITY

Tracey Turner

Åsa Gilland

KINGFISHER
LONDON & NEW YORK

For Toby – T.T.
To Nico and Linnea – Å.G.

A Raspberry Book
Art direction & design: Sidonie Beresford-Browne
Additional design: Sophie Wilcox & Peter Clayman
Text: Tracey Turner
Illustration: Åsa Gilland

KINGFISHER
LONDON & NEW YORK

Text and design copyright © Raspberry Books Ltd 2021, 2023
First published 2021 in the United States by Kingfisher,
This edition published 2023 in the United States by Kingfisher
120 Broadway, New York, NY 10271
Kingfisher is an imprint of
Macmillan Children's Books, London

Distributed in the U.S. and Canada by Macmillan,
120 Broadway, New York, NY 10271

EU representative: Macmillan Publishers Ireland Ltd, 1st Floor,
The Liffey Trust Centre, 117-126 Sheriff Street Upper, Dublin 1, D01 YC43.

Library of Congress Cataloging-in-Publication Data has been applied for.

ISBN 978-0-7534-7868-4

Kingfisher books are available for special promotions and premiums.
For details contact: Special Markets Department, Macmillan, 120 Broadway,
New York, NY 10271

For more information, please visit
www.kingfisherbooks.com

Printed in China
1 3 5 7 9 8 6 4 2
1TR/0523/RV/WKT/140WF

CONTENTS

Introducing . . . Everybody! 4

We Are All Unique 6

What's the Same, and
  What's Different? 8

Girls and Boys 10

Families 12

Brothers and Sisters 14

Adoption and Fostering 16

Autism Spectrum 18

How We Learn 20

Learning Differences 22

Learning Disabilities 24

Physical Disabilities 26

Seeing and Hearing 28

Our Ethnic Groups 30

Another Country 32

Different Cultures 34

Be Kind 36

I Want to Be 38

Belonging 40

We Are All Human 42

Glossary 44

Index 46

Thank You 48

INTRODUCING...EVERYBODY!

Welcome to our school! It's the start of a busy day. Children are arriving with their parents and guardians, and teachers are outside to meet them. Maybe it's like your school, or it might be a little different.

SCHOOL

4

WE ARE ALL UNIQUE

There's no one else quite like you in the world. Every single one of us is unique, not just in the way we look, but in the way we feel and see the world, and in our likes and dislikes. Even identical twins don't have the same personality.

Some people prefer to be with other people most of the time.

I'd be with my friends **ALL** the time if I could.

I find it hard to be in a big group of people.

I love playing with my friends, but I like being by myself too.

Watch this!

Some of us are shy . . .

I feel a little nervous when I meet people for the first time. Sometimes I feel shy at a party even if I know everyone.

. . . others love to be the center of attention.

BUDD
BEN

We can be good at different things,
and we all have different interests.

LOVES
READING
AND
ANIMALS

LIKES
SOCCER,
SWIMMING,
AND MUSIC

ANIMALS
OF
THE WORLD

GREAT AT
CHESS AND
TELLING
JOKES

We're different from
one another, but we can find
many things in common. And
there's one thing we should
all try to be . . .

KIND TO
EACH OTHER!

WHAT'S THE SAME, AND WHAT'S DIFFERENT?

At our school, we have **TONS** of things in common.

We like drawing and painting.

We LOVE soccer!

We play a game we made up called hide-and-sneak.

You have to sneak up on the seeker!

We like dressing up!

We both love music and dancing and have the same favorite band.

You can have a lot in common but be different from one another in other ways.

Our parents are from different countries and have different religions, but we're friends and so are our families.

We all go camping together! I love his dad's samosas, and he likes Mom's blini.

I love soccer and he hates it, but we're best friends.

We both enjoy reading, swimming, and video games.

ALL of us have something else in common too. We all have the same feelings at different times—we might be worried, happy, frightened, excited, sad, angry, calm, grumpy, confident . . . and there are MANY other feelings.

GIRLS AND BOYS

The world is often divided up into women and girls, men and boys, but some people don't fit into either of those groups.

ANDY   JASPER   NATTY   SASHA   GRACE

Physical differences on the outside of our bodies, as well as differences inside our bodies, all make up a complicated scale, with "male" on one side and "female" on the other. A lot of people are "intersex"—they fall somewhere in the middle.

"Gender identity" means whether you feel like a girl or a boy, or neither, or a mixture. People who don't think of themselves as girls or boys are "nonbinary."

My foster mother's friend Steph is nonbinary. They're called "they" instead of "he" or "she." Here's what Steph says . . .

WHAT STEPH SAYS ABOUT HE/SHE/THEY

★ You can express who you are by the words that are used to describe you. Examples are he/him, she/her, they/them— these are pronouns. My pronouns are they/them, but some nonbinary people use he/him, she/her, or xe/xem.

★ When you meet someone for the first time, it's polite to ask which pronouns they use and tell them yours—you can't tell how someone feels inside by looking at them.

★ If you don't know someone's pronouns and can't ask, it's best to use "they" until they tell you or you can ask.

★ Using the wrong pronouns can hurt someone's feelings. Your pronouns are up to YOU!

It wasn't so long ago that there were rules about what you could do depending on whether you were male or female. In some countries, there still are.

OWAIN   PAUL   NADEEM   MABEL

Only men could vote in the old days!

My granny taught me to knit—but she says only girls knitted when she was little!

I'm glad I don't have to wear a skirt.

I love playing soccer. Girls are great at sports!

There are no such things as boys' toys and girls' toys, and the same goes for games, books, hobbies, and other activities. All children (and grown-ups) can choose to read, play, and do the same things.

Some people have ideas about how we should behave according to our gender. They might say things like "Men are strong" and "Women are gentle." But you don't have to behave a particular way because of your sex or gender. You're free to be who you want to be.

FAMILIES

Families come in all kinds of different
shapes and sizes—just like people.

I have two moms,
one brother, and one sister.

I live in a children's home with
lots of other children. The
staff take care of us.

I have a mom, a dad,
and a sister.

This is my foster
family. I've lived
with them for
two years.

I have two dads
and one baby brother.

We live with Granny
and Grandpa.

And me and
my dad in
mine!

It's me and my mom
in my family.

There are all of these ways to be
a family and PLENTY MORE.
The important thing is that you
feel safe, loved, and cared for.

My family is my mom
and stepdad, who I live with
some of the time, and my
dad, who I live with the
rest of the time.

13

BROTHERS AND SISTERS

Some families are big, and some are small.
Not everyone has brothers and sisters, and not
all brothers and sisters get along!

My sister Natty is sassy and funny. She's always kind if I hurt myself.

Mia is the best sister. But she doesn't like it when I copy her!

Sometimes we're a band!

Arguments are bound to happen—they're a natural part of being close to other people.

ADOPTION AND FOSTERING

Not all children are born into their family.
Some become a member of a family later on.

Adopted children were born to parents who weren't able to take care of them—there can be all kinds of different reasons why. The adoptive parents wanted to give a child or children a loving family home, and so they became the child's family instead.

> I was really little when I first met Mom and Dad.

> Fudge and Buttons are part of the family too!

Foster children live with a family that's been chosen to give them a safe, caring place to stay while their birth family or other guardians aren't able to take care of them. Foster parents do all the same things other parents do.

This is Elmo the cat!

Our foster parents are Al and Kate. Their son, Felix, is our foster brother.

Foster children often keep in touch with their birth family. Sometimes adopted children do too. But it might not be possible for birth families to be in touch, for various reasons.

AUTISM SPECTRUM

Some people are autistic. You can't tell just by looking at them.

I'm autistic—I'm on the autism spectrum.

Me too! We experience the world in different ways from most people.

All autistic people are different from one another, just like other people aren't all exactly the same. Autism covers a big range—or "spectrum"—of people. But here are some of the things they might have in common:

SOME THINGS ABOUT AUTISTIC PEOPLE BY EVIE

SOME OF US MIGHT . . .

★ be good at coming up with new ideas

★ **pay attention to detail more than most people**

★ find groups and busy places difficult or upsetting

★ **worry more than most people**

★ shout and lash out when we're very upset—this is a meltdown; or we might not respond—this is a shutdown

★ **find it hard to understand language that doesn't have a clear meaning—like some jokes**

★ really dislike being touched—ask first!—and certain noises, smells, or textures that most people don't mind

★ **not like to look people in the eye**

★ tend to see things as either good or bad, not in between

★ **find changes very difficult, even if it's a small change like a school assembly being at a different time**

★ use sign language or letter boards instead of speaking

SOME THINGS PEOPLE GET WRONG ABOUT AUTISTIC PEOPLE
~~~ BY MO ~~~

★ **We're all really good at math and computer science.**
   We can be good (or bad) at many different things.

★ **We don't care about other people, and we don't feel emotions.**
   We feel the same emotions as everyone else—and we feel them really
   strongly. We might not show them in the same way as most other people.

★ **We don't want friends.**
   Many of us do want friends. Some are happy on their own.
   ## JUST ASK!

Being autistic can be difficult sometimes.

But it can also be awesome! It's part of who I am.

Plenty of funny, caring, fascinating, wonderful people are
autistic. It can be hard to live in a world that other people
experience differently from you, and where things aren't
designed with you in mind. So autistic people might need
understanding and support. Finding out more about the
autistic spectrum means we can all help one another.

HOW WE LEARN

All of us find some things easier to learn than others, whether it's tying our shoelaces, reading, or telling the time. We all need extra help sometimes.

It took me forever to understand coding!

I'm good at math, but I don't like art.

My favorite subject is PE, but spelling is hard.

We all learn in different ways.

I find it easier to remember things if I read about them in books or on a screen.

I learn best when I'm listening to someone talk.

BIOLOGY

OWAIN

You can ask your teacher to help you figure out which kind of learner you are. You might be a mixture of different kinds.

It's harder for me to learn by listening or reading—I learn best by doing.

I like to work as part of a team.

I'd rather work on my own.

School suits some children better than others.

I don't go to school. My mom and dad teach me at home instead.

I love school, but my sister doesn't.

However we learn, we can all teach each other something.

LEARNING DIFFERENCES

Some people find certain things difficult to learn. Like autistic people, their brains work slightly differently from the average, so they learn in a slightly different way.

I'm dyslexic, which means I can find some ways of learning difficult.

Some dyslexic people find it hard to read, write, and spell, but other dyslexic people are really good at it! Lots of dyslexic people are creative.

I'm OK at reading, but I find it hard to do things in order or to remember a list I've just been told. I'm good at telling stories, and I want to be a writer when I grow up.

I need help learning numbers because I have dyscalculia. Clocks and money are really confusing!

Dyscalculia means having problems understanding numbers. A lot of children find math hard, but not all of them have dyscalculia.

I have ADHD, which means attention deficit hyperactivity disorder. Whew! I find concentrating hard and need help to focus in class. Sometimes moving helps me listen.

These learning differences don't stop children from doing well at school, as long as they can learn in ways that suit them.

It's a good thing that there are differences in the way people's brains work—it means there's a mixture of points of view and ideas. Otherwise, the world would be a much less interesting place!

LEARNING DISABILITIES

If you have a learning disability, it means you need help to learn. You might need help with other things too, like getting dressed.

HELLO!

GOODBYE

THANK YOU

PLEASE

BOOK

HOUSE

Everyone with Down syndrome has a learning disability of some kind, but everyone's needs are different. There are other conditions that can mean people need help with learning too.

I have Down syndrome. I needed help to learn to speak, but now I have trouble staying quiet! I have help with lessons in the classroom.

Sometimes people are impatient when I need time, and I feel bad when that happens. My friends are nice, though!

Learning disabilities can mean that people take longer to learn new things. They might need extra help to do the things they enjoy, and use special equipment to help them learn.

PHYSICAL DISABILITIES

Lots of people have a physical disability that can affect the way they live and what they do. As long as buildings are designed with everyone's needs in mind—like having wide doorways and ramps—physically disabled people can move around and do many of the things they want to.

Getting around is easy here because the school has ramps and an elevator.

Life would be easier if there were more ramps and wider doorways in the world. Sometimes there's a nice wide doorway and a ramp to get into a store, but then I can't reach the shelves!

Being physically disabled might affect people in other ways.

Sometimes people talk to my family or friends instead of to me—I can hear and talk, so it's annoying!

People who don't know me might stare.

It's not always obvious when someone has a disability.

Mom has an invisible disability—you can't see she has chronic fatigue syndrome. Sometimes, people don't understand that she needs to use disabled facilities.

27

SEEING AND HEARING

If you can't see or hear very well, it can affect how you live too.

Some people have hearing loss as well as vision loss.

Most "blind" people are partially sighted, like me—we can see a little. We don't all have guide dogs, but this is mine—her name's Molly. My granny is partially sighted too, and she uses a cane to get around.

LARGE PRINT PUZZLES

LARGE PRINT PUZZLES

CROSSWORDS RIDDLES AND PUZZLES

Writing you can touch, called Braille, helps partially sighted people, as do large-print books.

Not all service dogs are guide dogs for people with vision loss—there are hearing dogs, dogs that can help if someone has a seizure, and many more.

Deaf people can choose the language they use. Some have implants inside their ears when they're young so that they grow up able to hear and speak, and some wear hearing aids.

We might use sign language as well.

You don't have to be able to hear and speak to communicate!

Other Deaf people use only sign language to communicate and don't think of deafness as a disability at all.

Captions on screens, as well as apps that turn speech into written words, also help people with hearing loss.

OUR ETHNIC GROUPS

Our different skin colors are one of the outward signs of the ethnic group we belong to.

The many ethnic groups in the world are sometimes put into big categories, including Black, Asian, or white (there are MANY more). Each group has its own history.

I have a mixture of Bangladeshi and American heritage, so my family has two histories.

My grandparents came here from Jamaica more than 50 years ago. I love being a third-generation Jamaican!

It's good to find people who look like you in books, movies, and television. But often the mixture of different skin tones and ethnicities in the real world isn't shown on screen or on the page—at least, not nearly enough.

My family are Romani. Sometimes people say unkind things about us.

The ethnic group you come from should never have anything to do with how you're treated. But some people face racism—untrue and unfair ideas and judgments about different ethnic groups. This causes a LOT of harm.

Racism isn't always an obvious insult. And sometimes people don't realize they're being racist. But it always feels horrible to be judged because of your ethnicity, skin color, language, accent, or anything else!

It all adds up to one great big WRONG!

EVERYONE SHOULD BE TREATED EQUALLY

Racism in the United States is hundreds of years old. European settlers displaced American Indians, and Black people were enslaved. Many ethnic groups have been discriminated against throughout our country's history.

If someone's racist to you or someone else, tell them it's wrong if you can, and tell a trusted grown-up about it.

ANOTHER COUNTRY

There are almost 200 countries—or nations—in the world. People move from one to another for different reasons. Sometimes children go to school and have their classes in a completely new language.

My dad came here from Sri Lanka to work as a doctor. I was six and didn't know much English. Now I know a lot!

Families might move to a different part of the world to be with other relatives, for a better job or way of life, or because their own country isn't a safe place. Or just for an adventure!

I miss my grandparents and my cousins in Poland, but we visit every summer. People here are mostly kind and patient when I don't know words.

POLAND

I have two nationalities —Korean and American. I was born here but speak both languages.

Mom is from Mexico, Dad is from France. We speak three languages in our house! I speak English the most.

It can be lonely if you move to a new country, especially at first. Everything is new—sights, smells, sounds, and tastes. You might stand out because you're just learning the language everyone else speaks all the time. It helps if everyone is understanding, friendly, and welcoming.

33

DIFFERENT CULTURES

There's a wide variety of beliefs and traditions, manners, food, and styles of dress—all the things that make up different cultures. There are all kinds at our school, which means there's a lot to learn and always something to celebrate.

Here are some things the children like best about their own cultures.

Mom, Granny, and Grandpa come from Wales, in Britain. They tell Welsh stories and sing Welsh songs, and the whole family roots for the Welsh rugby team!

My family is Muslim. I have many aunts, uncles, and cousins, and we all support each other. I love the food my dhadi (grandmother) makes, especially her delicious mitai (sweets) for Eid.

My family is Jewish. I love the High Holy Days, when we celebrate Rosh Hashanah and Yom Kippur, because everyone gets together to celebrate.

My great-grandpa is from Ghana and plays Ghanaian music on his trumpet.

We celebrate Lunar New Year in January or February with fireworks and parties. I get money in red envelopes!

It's fascinating to find out about other cultures as well as our own—learning about them is fun and shows how we are all connected. We can all learn from one another's cultures.

BE KIND

Sometimes people say that words can't hurt you. But they can! Words are powerful—unkind words can hurt and leave scars you can't see that can last a long time. But kind words can spread happiness.

Everyone wants to feel good about themselves. You might feel happy that you sing in a choir, or you're good at chess. Sometimes people try to make themselves feel good by making someone else feel bad, so that they think they're better than the other person. They often target people who look or behave differently from them.

People might say terrible things without meaning to—maybe they're repeating something they heard someone else say. But it still has the same effect.

I still feel upset.

It doesn't matter if someone says it was "just a joke."

Jokes are only jokes if everyone finds them funny.

Unkind words can make people feel miserable and bad about themselves. They'll start to think that the world isn't a fun and safe place. If someone's unkind to you or someone else, tell a grown-up you trust. And always remember . . .

BE KIND

I WANT TO BE...

Everyone has hopes and dreams about their future lives.

I want to be a baker and work at a café.

I want to win an Olympic medal for swimming.

I want to travel the world.

I want to travel to space!

I have absolutely no idea what I want to do when I'm a grown-up!

Me neither!

I want to live in the country.

I want to be an actor. Or a teacher. Or maybe a singer . . .

I want to be president.

It's fun to think about what you want to do when you grow up, but it doesn't matter if you don't know. There's plenty of time. You'll probably change your mind a lot!

BELONGING

Feeling that we belong is important to all of us as human beings. Everyone wants to be valued and listened to, and to be part of a group, or of many different groups.

I'm part of my family, my school, and my basketball team.

Helping is part of belonging too. At school teachers give out jobs. At home there are many things to do to help.

Me and my brothers feed the rabbits, set and clear the table . . .

. . . help put away groceries, and water the plants.

Whatever you're like—
whether you . . .

can do a
cartwheel

were born in a
different country

play the piano

have a disability

find it hard to
make friends

are Chinese-American
or Cuban-American
or Italian-American

have a really
loud laugh

write stories

worry a lot

flap your hands
when you're excited

. . . you are unique and wonderful. You don't need to
change the way you are to try to fit in—if you did that,
it would make you uncomfortable and sad. Being
accepted and loved for who you are makes you happy.

41

WE ARE ALL HUMAN

There are BILLIONS of wonderful ways to be human—as many ways as there are people. The amazing variety of people is something to celebrate. Variety is part of what makes us human!

Differences make our lives richer and more interesting—they show us new ideas, open our eyes to other ways of life, and help us understand other people.

... abilities and disabilities

It's good that we THINK differently ...

... and religions

... and have different cultures

42

43

GLOSSARY

ADHD: stands for attention deficit hyperactivity disorder, a condition that affects behavior. People with ADHD might find it hard to sit still and concentrate, and they might find that movement helps them focus, but the condition affects everyone differently.

adoption: is a way of providing a safe, loving family for children who can't live with their birth parents. Adoptive parents are responsible for the child or children they adopt.

autism: means that people experience the world differently from most other people. It covers a very broad range and is different for each autistic person.

Braille: is an alphabet that is read by touch, useful for people with vision loss.

chronic fatigue syndrome (CFS): is a condition that means people are very tired a lot of the time, even when they've rested. There might be other symptoms too.

Deafness: people with hearing loss are often described as "deaf." Deaf people (with a capital "D") who are members of the Deaf culture communicate primarily in sign language and have a strong sense of community.

Down syndrome: people with this condition all have some level of learning disability, and some might have delays in their physical development. Every person with Down syndrome is completely unique.

dyscalculia: is a learning difficulty that affects how people learn numbers and math.

44

dyslexia: is a learning difficulty that can affect how people learn to read and write.

fostering: is a way of providing a safe, loving family for children who can't live with their birth parents, by placing them with foster parents who take care of them for a period of time.

gender identity: is how people feel about their gender—girl, boy, both, or neither.

High Holy Days: Jewish holidays in which Rosh Hashanah and Yom Kippur are celebrated.

intersex: intersex people are born with physical characteristics that don't fit what is traditionally considered to be male or female.

Lunar New Year: is the beginning of a calendar year with months that relate to the cycles of the Moon. It is celebrated in East Asia and is sometimes called Chinese New Year.

nonbinary: people who are nonbinary don't feel the genders "male" or "female" are right for them. They might feel like both genders, or neither.

pronoun: is a word that takes the place of a noun—for example, using "it" instead of "table." Personal pronouns include "she," "they," and "he."

racism: untrue and unfair ideas and judgments about different ethnic groups.

service dog: a trained dog that can assist people with vision loss, hearing loss, or various other conditions.

sign language: a visual language that uses signs made with the hands and body and facial expressions.

xe/xem: people can choose to use the pronouns xe/xem (pronounced "ze/zem") instead of she/her, he/him, or they/them.

INDEX

ADHD (attention deficit hyperactivity disorder) 23
adopted children 16, 17
arguments 15
autism spectrum 18–19

belonging 40–41
birth families 17
Braille 28
brothers and sisters 14–15

celebrations 34, 35
children's homes 12
chronic fatigue syndrome 27
cultures 34–35

Deaf people 29
Down syndrome 24
dyscalculia 22
dyslexia 22

equal treatment 31
ethnic groups 30–31

families 12–17
feelings, hurting someone's 10, 36, 37
food 9, 34
foster children 12, 15, 17

gender identity 10–11
girls and boys 10–11
grandparents 13
guide dogs 28

he/she/they 10
hearing aids 29
hearing dogs 28
hearing loss 28, 29
helping 40
homeschooling 21
hopes and dreams 38–39

intersex people 10

kindness 7, 36–37

languages 32, 33
learning 20–25
learning differences 22–23
learning disabilities 24–25
likes and dislikes 6–9

male and female 10, 11

nationalities 32-33

nonbinary people 10

partially sighted people 28

personality and interests 6-9

physical disabilities 26-29

pronouns 10

racism 30, 31

ramps and doorways 26, 27

religions 9, 34, 35

Romani 30

school 4-5, 21, 23, 24, 26,
    32, 34, 40

seizures 28

service dogs 28

sign language 18, 29

skin colors 30, 31

slaves 31

stepfamilies 13, 15

teachers 21, 40

twins 6

unique 6, 41

unkind words 36, 37

variety 42-43

vision loss 28

women and men 10-11

THANK YOU

Thanks to Beth Cox, Inclusion and Equality Consultant, whose insights were invaluable.

Thanks also to Inclusive Minds for introducing us to their network of Inclusion Ambassadors. We couldn't have made this book without the help of the following Inclusion Ambassadors, who have been kind enough to share their knowledge and experience:

Hannah Ahmed

Jessica Chaikof

Rachel Faturoti

Rebecca Heyes

Ciara McDonagh

Syeda Ferdushi Mohshin

Hayley Newman, Mia, and Natty from Downs Side Up

Jo Ross-Barrett

Emma Zipfel